Best Year Ever

Best Year Ever

For When You're Ready To Stop Making Excuses And Start Having The Year (And Life) You Deserve

THOUGHT CATALOG

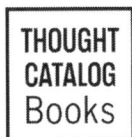

THOUGHT CATALOG Books

BROOKLYN, NY

**THOUGHT
CATALOG
Books**

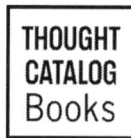

Published by Thought Catalog Books, a division of The Thought & Expression Co., Williamsburg, Brooklyn. Founded in 2010, Thought Catalog is a website and imprint dedicated to your ideas and stories. We publish fiction and non-fiction from emerging and established writers across all genres. For general information and submissions: manuscripts@thoughtcatalog.com.

First edition, 2017

ISBN: 978-1542781787

Printed and bound in the United States.

10 9 8 7 6 5 4 3 2 1

Contents

How To Ruin Your Year (Before It's Even Started)

Kim Quindlen

Focus on loving others so strongly that you forget to love yourself. Neglect yourself long enough that you start to accept the kind of love that is less than you deserve, because you start to believe that it's the best you'll ever get.

Let yourself get bogged down by never-ending emails, and work deadlines, and commitments on top of commitments. Convince yourself that this is what makes you important, that this is the only way you have worth. Focus on doing, doing, doing–instead of being. Confuse this amount of stress and business in your everyday existence to be the same thing as living your life to the fullest, as being happy.

Decide that even if you're unhappy, it's too late to change anything, too late to try anything else.

Too late to leave your job for the career that you've dreamed about from the beginning, the career that feels right in your gut and makes you happiest. Too late to take up a new hobby, or to learn a new skill, or to show up to that dance class and see if you 'have something' like you always thought you might. Too late to walk away from the relationship with that person who makes you miserable and to try to make it on your own for a while. Decide that it's too late, too late, too late. That this is the life you've made for yourself and you have to accept it as is.

Fail to ask for help when you truly need it, especially from those who truly care about you and who would drop every single thing in their life if they knew that you needed them. Tell yourself that you have to suck it up, that you have to suffer silently. Decide that telling your loved ones that you need them would make you a 'burden' and that instead, you just need to white-knuckle it and be alone, that asking for help is for other, weaker people. That you can't need help and be strong at the same time.

Walk through your year asleep. Do everything you can to avoid being alone with your own thoughts. Run away from silence. Scroll, scroll, scroll. Make everything loud–the tv, your music, your phone, your conversations, your own voice. Don't try meditation or focused breathing or reading or a break from your phone on your commute or anything else that would bring you into too close of contact with your own self.

Ruin your year, before it's even started, by just getting by.

Accept love that is less than you deserve, just because it's there. Keep working at a job you hate. Stay in that relationship with that person who mistreats you. Be a mediocre friend. Avoid any sense of responsibility. Avoid things that are intimidating. Avoid good love. Avoid yourself. Avoid the happiness that you truly deserve, because 'getting by' is at least a little less scary.

17 People Share Their Super Honest New Year's Resolutions

Ari Eastman

1. "I want to cut down on drinking. I don't like who I become when I'm drunk, way too impulsive and obnoxious. It's not cute to be the woman in her late 20s still acting like she's at a frat party. And it would be nice to not have monster hangovers."

—Luisa, 28

2. "I've been in a job that makes me super unhappy for a while now. I keep saying I'm going to look for other work, but years later, I'm still in something that feels soul sucking. Change is a thing I've always struggled with, so I know part of what holds me back is fear. But I'm so tired of the same monotonous routine. I'm sending my resume out in the New Year."

—Alyssa, 31

3. "I'm working out, but ditching the scale. I've been approaching fitness wrong and I think if I stop looking at myself as a work-in-progress that has to hit a specific number, I'm going to be much more successful with getting healthy."

—Dee, 24

4. "I want to work on my relationship with my dad. We've been pretty estranged since I was a teenager, but lately, I've been reminded how fragile life is. It gives me a lot of anxiety and I'm terrified of him rejecting me or the woman I've become, but I owe it to both of us to work on it. He's my only dad. I don't want to look back and regret not trying."

—Elizabeth, 29

5. "I'm letting go of my ex. I mean, I think I've let just his memory haunt me for so long, I'm almost sad to fully bury the idea of us. But I know I'm never going to really move forward until I allow myself to move on."

—Dylan, 25

6. "I want to see my favorite band in concert. Is that a dumb resolution?"

—Melania, 20

7. "Therapy. My one and only resolution; I'm finally seeking treatment for depression. I've lived in denial the past year and it's time to actually get help so I can become the best, healthiest version of myself."

—Scott, 27

8. "I can be kind of a flake and tend to cancel plans I make. I can't promise that I'm going to turn into some social butterfly, but I'm going to push myself to be accountable and available for the people in my life."

—Nellie, 24

9. "I'm gonna sleep with the hot barista I've been crushing on forever. Or at the very least, ask him out."

—Zora, 24

10. "I'm going to practice saying yes to opportunities. Do things out of the norm that I wouldn't usually do. I want the New Year to be a year of growth and adventure, and that starts by saying yes to things!"

—Nora, 23

11. "Going to attend weekly open mics. I'm a musician, but I rarely play these days. I'm not really expecting to make a living off it, but it's something I'm passionate about. I figure if I make a schedule and actually go perform, it can only help my mood and maybe link me with other creative-minded people."

—Darren, 26

12. "Blocking my shitty ex and not running back to him whenever he promises me he's changed. Because, shocker, he never does."

—Mary, 23

13. "I don't really believe in resolutions. Life happens and you slip up, and then make yourself feel shitty for just being human."

—Jason, 33

14. "I'm getting a dog. And yes, this is the best resolution of all time."

—Calista, 27

15. "I'm going to try online dating. I actually haven't ever been on a real date and as a 25-year-old, this makes me feel so behind everyone else. I have an issue with putting myself out there, so the prospect of dating is Hellish to me. But I'm gonna take the first step to try and remedy that. Even if it's with something as lame as downloading Tinder."

—Jess, 25

16. "I bought a one-way ticket to a city 2,000 miles away to start over."

—Elaine, 29

17. "I'm giving myself permission to fall in love again after my divorce. Even if it means I end up hurt…again. I'm giving myself a chance to find out what else exists out there."

—Derek, 28

24 Things You Need To Give Yourself A Little More Credit For This Year

Heidi Priebe

1. All the pain you've pulled yourself through.

When our lives go off the rails, we tend to slip into survival mode–doing whatever needs to be done to change our situation and then moving on from it as swiftly as possible. We scarcely stop to acknowledge just how much strength and tenacity it takes to keep us going through those times. This year, make a point to acknowledge the person who wiped your tears, pulled you through your toughest hours and got you to where you are today. Because that person's you. And they deserve some thanks.

2. All of the times you've stayed strong for other people.

When shit hits the fan, it's an unspoken rule that at least one person has to hold it together so that everyone else can fall apart. Start giving yourself some credit for all the times when that person's been you. It's a thankless but honorable role–and it's one that not everyone can handle.

3. The failures you tried for in the first place.

We lament endlessly over our downfalls but we rarely stop to pat ourselves on the back for actually having gone after what we wanted. It doesn't always work out–that's a necessary consequence of taking risks. But in the long run, becoming the kind of person who takes those risks is a much greater feat than any one individual failure could ever eclipse.

4. The work you do just to keep yourself alive.

The job you don't love, but work anyway. The side hustle you're keeping afloat. The education you keep hacking away at, knowing it will lead you to better things or the student loans you're dutifully paying down. We rarely give ourselves credit for the 'bare minimum' behaviours we engage in to keep ourselves afloat, but in the long run, they make all the difference. And they're necessary evils that not everybody is up to fighting.

5. The second chances that you have granted.

Not all second chances are granted out of weakness. In most cases, it takes genuine strength to understand a situation from someone else's side and allow them a chance at redemption–knowing that you're risking personal pain in the process. Give yourself some credit for the people you've shown mercy to. You are deciding to be the bigger person that so many other people couldn't be for you.

6. The mornings when you don't feel like getting out of bed but do anyway.

Some people lose this battle more than they win it. If you're always (or almost always) able to pull yourself up to face the day, even when you don't want to, you're probably doing better than you think.

7. The brilliant people you've brought into and kept in your life.

The people you have in your life aren't a coincidence: they're a direct reflection of the energy you're putting out into the world. So if you're surrounded by some top-notch human beings, chances are you're pretty solid company yourself.

8. All of the unhealthy shit you've walked away from.

Recognizing that a job, relationship, situation or thought pattern is toxic is infinitely harder than most of us realize. Any time you're able to identify something that's unhealthy for you and make the conscious choice to remove it from your life, you're a step ahead of most of the population.

9. All of the healthy relationships you've nurtured.

We spend so much time focused on the relationships that have fallen apart that we rarely take the time to appreciate the ones that haven't. This year, pause to consider the friendship you have that have spanned decades, the coworkers you've turned into confidants and the family members you've grown steadily closer to as you've aged. Chances are, your life is bursting with healthy relationships–you just don't stop to fully consider or appreciate them.

10. The ambitions you haven't yet risen to.

You may not be living your dream right now, but the fact that you even have one speaks volumes. Don't discount the power of having a clear-cut goal to work towards–positive motivation is powerful. Having faith that you can get to where you want to go is so often half the battle.

11. The achievements you've collected in the past.

It's an unfortunate consequence of the human condition that our failures tend to stand out more prominently than our triumphs. This year, when you look over your past achievements, take a moment to reflect on how many challenges you've risen to and how many trials you've overcome. Chances are you have a long list of accomplishments and feats–you just keep forgetting to give yourself credit for them.

12. The well-meaning intentions you harbour.

Here's the deal: we all screw up sometimes. We all turn left when we should have turned right and we all make mistakes that we hold ourselves accountable for, sometimes for far too long.

But in the midst of that, it's important to pause and consider not just what actions we took, but what our intentions were. A lot of the time, we had perfectly good intentions when we made our mistakes. And those intentions count for something. They remind us who we want to be, and who we want to be matters.

13. The determination you harness.

Take a minute. Look at all the times you've gotten knocked down in life. And then look at all of the times you've gotten back up. If those numbers are even roughly equivalent, chances are you're doing just fine. At the end of the day, it's determination that gets you through, far more than your skills or abilities. Having a strong sense of it means you also have more power than you know.

14. The support you've given others at their worst.

It's easy to love someone when things are going well. What

takes true strength and endurance is loving someone through the rough spots in their lives—the times that make them into small and miserable versions of themselves. Give yourself some credit for the people you've seen through the worst–that's the mark of a real friend. The kind of friend we all need.

15. The mistakes you have realized.

Nobody gets through life without messing a few things up along the way. But a lot of people get through life without ever taking accountability for what they've messed up. If you're able to do so–and to repent for the things you've done wrong–you're ahead of the game. You have a self-awareness that most people do not possess.

16. The love you don't question.

The people you support without hesitation. The people whose sides you rush to when things go wrong. The love you dole out without a second thought–that kind of devotion is rare. And if it's a love that you're actively practicing, you're probably making a much stronger impact on the people around you than you realize.

17. The love you do question.

Just as important as the love that comes naturally to you is the love that doesn't. The family members you've struggled to reconcile with. The relationships you've worked hard to salvage. The love that you continue to choose when times are tough–all of it says infinitely more about you than the love that you choose when the sailing's smooth. This year, take the time to appreciate the relationships you have fostered and salvaged against all odds.

18. Your optimism when things are grim.

When the cards are stacked against us, giving into self-pity and pessimism is the easiest thing in the world. Remaining optimistic and headstrong throughout the storms that life sends our way is an immensely underrated quality. And it's one that you're probably not giving yourself enough credit for.

19. The humour you can shed on tough situations.

The ability to laugh at oneself is a truly underrated one. If you are able to find any semblance of humor within the pain and heartache that life sends your way, you're the exact kind of person the world needs more of. Laughter is a healing quality. And those who can dole it out are absolutely irreplaceable.

20. The values you refuse to compromise on.

Many of our values shift and evolve over the course of our lives. But a select few remain consistent, and we rarely stop to give ourselves props for holding true to those. Those are almost always the values we intuitively know to be right. And to remain true to what we know to be right over the course of an entire lifetime is definitely no easy feat.

21. The lofty pipe dream you're still holding onto.

Being wildly idealistic is often a frowned upon quality–but it shouldn't be. In the words of George Bernard Shaw, "The reasonable man adapts himself to the world; the unreasonable one persists in trying to adapt the world to himself. Therefore all progress depends on the unreasonable man." Keeping your lofty dreams alive in a world of realists is a noble battle to fight–and those who win it are the ones who go on to make real changes.

22. The humility you practice when you need to.

The unglamorous jobs you work to support yourself while you pursue bigger dreams. The apologies you offer up when you know they're warranted. The hard, gritty work that you don't shy away from when you know you need to buckle down. Humility is an underrated quality in our current society and it's one that takes you further than you probably give it credit for.

23. All the times you've proven yourself wrong.

Think of all the people, situations, failures, misgivings and mistakes that it once felt like you'd never get over. And yet here you are, still living. Still growing. Still striving and thriving and carrying on. You have proven yourself wrong an infinite number of times in the past and you will absolutely do so again in the future. Give yourself some credit for all of the odds you've already overcome.

24. The ways in which you've already changed for the better.

It's easy to become so focused on who we want to become that we forget about all the people we've been in the past–and all the ways in which we've already evolved into stronger, kinder, bolder versions of ourselves. This year, take a moment to consider not just where you want to go, but where you've been. And all the awesome changes you have already made for yourself.

6 Ways To Have A New Year, Same You, But With A Little Less Bullshit

Andrea Neski

Don't beat around the bush.

Do you really want to start off your new year repressing all your feelings? Life is significantly simpler when you say what is on your mind as clear and concisely as you can. Fear is usually what keeps people from really speaking their mind, but would you rather face your fears or deal with the consequences that will ultimately come from not telling people what the fuck is up? You have the right to tell people your opinion, how you feel about them and the things they're doing.

Stop feeling sorry for yourself.

All right, we get it, that guy you've been obsessing over for a month doesn't like you back. Your best friend left you at the bar to go hang out with some random guy she's known for five minutes. You really fucked up that important test because you could not stop binge watching *Grey's Anatomy*. Shit happens. Shit happens to *everyone*. Shit even happens to that girl in your Psych class that manages to dress immaculately and brush her hair for class every single day. Sometimes things happen to you, and sometimes things happen *because* of you. Either way, you need to deal. So take a moment, get pissed, get sad, but then know when to get over it.

Don't let anyone tell you your feelings don't matter.

Every once in awhile you feel things and you can't even understand them. They come on so suddenly and strongly that you just can't shake these feelings. To put it simply, there are two types of emotions: good and bad ones. Do you ever wake up and you're just a little happier and filled with all those good emotions? You finally got that bug problem under control in your house, that weird smell that was coming from your fridge has resolved itself, and your 8 AM class got canceled. It's going to be a good day.

But then your roommate comes home and she's feeling all the bad emotions for the fifth day in a row for who knows what reason. Here's the thing: yeah, it sucks and she's annoying and a bitch, but just as much as you have the right to feel all those good emotions, she has every right to feel however she does, too. As corny as it sounds, everyone's feelings should matter—good and bad—simply because they feel them.

Do not put up with shitty people in your life. Period. End of story.

Do you really want this year to be the year where you go to yet another Sunday brunch with that girl who has never really listened to anything you've ever said, doesn't know how to be wrong? That girl who turns her nose up at anyone and everyone that is different; the girl who can't even say 'please' or 'thank you' to a waiter? I'm going to give you the answer here: hell no. Everyone comes into your life for a reason, but sometimes that reason is to teach you your worth as a person.

Nothing in your life is going to change unless you do.

If you keep doing the same things with the same people at the same places every day and you're not happy, what do you expect? If you are unhappy, change something. Quit that shitty job where your old sweaty boss is always hitting on you. Move out of that terrible apartment next to that crazy cat lady that smells like a combination of death and cheese. Leave your terrible relationship that hasn't been fulfilling your needs for a long time. Nothing in your life will change unless you do; you are in total control of your own life.

Uncomfortable and new are a great combination.

Doing new things is scary; it's even scarier when you have to do it alone. So when you're ready to make a change, do some new things. It's all right that you feel uncomfortable and all around pretty awkward. Let's face it, the first time you go to that hot yoga class at your gym that you've been saying you're going to try for months but never do, it's not going to be pretty. It's probably not even going to be yoga.

But by the fifth class, you'll know that spot in the class that you like—just far enough away from the door, in perfect range of the ceiling fans—and you finally won't feel as awkward. Eventually awkward and uncomfortable will turn into you finding your way. Those little wins in life are the ones that will feel the best at the end of the day. When uncomfortable turns into being on a first-name basis with your yoga teacher, that is a win and you should be proud.

5

What Your New Year's Resolution Should Be In 5 Words, Based On Your Zodiac Sign

Kim Quindlen

Aries

(March 21st to April 19th)

Learn to appreciate stillness sometimes.

Taurus

(April 20th to May 21st)

To finally put yourself first.

Gemini

(May 22nd to June 21st)

Be *you*, whoever you are.

Cancer

(June 22nd to July 22nd)

Focus on *your* emotional needs.

Leo

(July 23rd to August 22nd)

Be open to new thinking.

Virgo

(August 23rd to September 22nd)

Stop worrying about trivial things.

Libra

(September 23rd to October 22nd)

To stick to your decisions.

Scorpio

(October 23rd to November 22nd)

Focus your energy towards positivity.

Sagittarius

(November 23rd to December 21st)

Take matters into your hands.

Capricorn

(December 22nd to January 20th)

Make room for your humor.

Aquarius

(January 21st to February 18th)

To give *everything* your all.

Pisces

(February 19th to March 20th)

Choose what you want, unapologetically.

6

The One-Sentence Reminder That Each Personality Type Needs For The New Year

Heidi Priebe

ENFP: You need roots just as much as you need wings.

INFP: That talent that you're afraid to show the world is probably exactly what the world needs.

ENFJ: Nobody is judging you as harshly as you are judging yourself.

INFJ: You don't have to have the entire course mapped out in order to take the first step.

ENTP: Whatever you are trying to control, controls you.

INTP: Sometimes the problem is not that you cannot find the answer, but that you are phrasing the questions incorrectly.

ENTJ: You can't always control your environment, but you CAN control your reaction to your environment.

INTJ: Your frustrations with the outer world are always a reflection of your frustrations with your inner world.

ESFP: Deep down, you know exactly what you want and how to get it—you just have to trust yourself enough to choose it.

ISFP: Don't worry so much about perfection—there is absolutely nothing less interesting than perfection.

ESFJ: The person who is the most deserving of your unconditional love and generosity is you.

ISFJ: The people you love want you to make yourself a priority.

ESTP: Boredom and routine are not fatal—they might even be helpful if used in moderation.

ISTP: When you can't work out the truth, listen to your intuition—it knows a thing or two, too.

ESTJ: Sometimes taking a break to recharge is, paradoxically, the most efficient move you can make.

ISTJ: Sometimes you just have to be the moral compass you want to see in the world.

You Don't Need A New Years Resolution, And Here's Why

Ashlee Schultz

Congratulations! You've survived last year. Welcome to the future.

The promise of a new year prompts us to take a good, hard look at ourselves and evaluate the choices we've made and are making with regard to the future. It's our nature to strive to be great–to do more, create more, and look at ourselves in a new, improved light. We all want to be the best versions of ourselves, whether we're conscious of it or not.

Even though we're capable of making life-altering changes at *any* time, the span of a fresh twelve months in a calendar year indulges our linear brain's need for measurable results. This is why nearly half the population make resolutions every year—and yet, only 8 percent manage to keep them. What's up with that?

Let's take a look at some of the top resolutions people made for this year:

- Lose weight
- Get organized
- Spend less, save more
- Fall in love
- Spend more time with family

Do you notice a theme among these resolutions?

They all indicate *lack*. There is nothing wrong with wanting to make changes in areas of health, lifestyle, finance, or relationships. Making positive changes in any of these areas would cater to improved well-being. But our attitude toward any area of our life is reflected in the language we use to describe it.

By changing our language, we can change our attitudes. By changing our attitudes, we shift from the negative (a state of lack because we think we *don't* have what we want) to the positive (our natural state of abundance).

Intending to lose weight indicates lack of appreciation for the body one already has. Getting organized indicates lack of control of possessions or success. Spending less and saving more indicates lack of money. Resolving to fall in love is indicative of being incomplete without someone else. Finally, resolving to spend more time with family suggests a lack of enough 'free time' to go around.

Of course, the resolutions listed above are obtainable and accessible with the passing of time. The problem with resolutions (and some big goals), and the reason why they often fail at providing the lasting change we'd like to see, is that we bust out of the gate gung-ho and ready to live a new, improved life...only to be let down when we don't see immediate change. Let down breeds let down, and lack breeds more lack. With enough verbal or mental negative repetition, we actually convince ourselves that our desires and goals are unobtainable. When we do so, we sink back into a state of hopelessness and quietly accept that we just aren't capable of creating the change we'd like to see.

But now that you understand that, you can go back to remembering that you're a creator, not a victim of circumstance.

You are capable of creating whatever positive change you'd like. There is nothing wrong with you.

I'm going to help you alter your resolution so that it is not only obtainable, but also immediate. *All you have to do is just be what you already are.*

First, let's change our language, which will change our attitudes, which will change our results.

Here are the same resolutions with altered language:

- ~~Lose weight~~ Be/stay active, healthy and fit
- ~~Get organized~~ Remember that the exterior is a reflection of the interior
- ~~Spend less, save more~~ Evaluate what it is I truly need
- Fall in love **with myself**

• ~~Spend more time with family~~ Remember that time is the currency of priority

Can you see the difference?

By shining a new light on any situation, the situation changes. When you change the way you look at things, the things you look at change.

To illustrate what I mean, I've elaborated a bit on each subject.

Health.

In seeing ourselves as beings who are naturally healthy and active, we begin to alter our choices to align with *who we really are.* There is no diet or exercise regime that is appropriate for everyone; the way we eat and exercise are byproducts of how we see ourselves. Drink water. Eat vegetables. Don't reach for a bottle of Tylenol every time you have a headache. Are you tired? Do you eat because you're hungry or because it's 9 AM and you always eat at 9 AM? What is habit, and what is instinct?

Listen to what your body asks you for. It developed itself for nine months before you even realized you were a conscious being. It knows what it's doing. Trust it. When you allow your body to call the shots, you negate resistance and, in turn, put complete faith in your ability to be healthy. In trusting your own ability to be well, you will begin to make conscious decisions to continue being well. It's the easiest thing in the world. You don't even have to *do* anything. Your natural state is health.

Well-being.

How about the state of your house, apartment, or bedroom? Do you feel refreshed and energized when you wake up, or do your eyes immediately dart to a pile of clothes on the floor and a bunch of stuff shoved on a shelf that you haven't touched in God knows how long? There is a Hermetic adage that is appropriate here: "as above, so below." *Our exterior environments are reflections of our inner environments.* Both mental and physical clutter are the same. We assume that holding onto things from the past will somehow bring us something sentimental and meaningful, as they serve as reminders from happy times in our lives. But are they also serving as anchors that keep us away from focusing on the present?

Whether it's an item or a memory, it's not beneficial for us to hold onto something because it may serve a purpose *what if or one day.* In tuning our attention away from the past and future, we are able to gauge what we need right now, and our ability to hold on or let go will naturally reflect that. Again, you don't have to do anything. You're already in a present state of clarity; it's only in reflecting on the chaos of the past or the fear of the future that we create confusion.

Finance.

When we think about what it is we truly need, we realize pretty quickly that we already have it. Pursuit of status, be it monetary or a position of power, blinds us to our relationship to the contented life that is already available. We're already living it!

Overvaluing possessions and accomplishments stems from our ego's fixation of getting *more*–wealth, belongings, status or the like. Rather than seeking more, practice gratitude for what you already have. The advice to "not do" and trust that all will settle perfectly into place may sound like a prescription for laziness, but I'm not saying to be passive and inactive. Rather, trusting the universe to provide your highest desires is allowing yourself to be guided by more than simple, ego-driven desires. How do we figure out our highest desires? Listen for what urges you onward, free from ego domination, and you'll paradoxically be more productive and engage in opportunities that will further you along your path of least resistance. When action is pure and selfless, everything settles into its own perfect place, and you will be amazed at the coincidences (miracles?) that converge for your benefit.

Again, it takes zero effort except to act according to your authentic, honest self.

Relationships/friendships.

I've heard love described as a fulfilling sense of completion. "He/she is my other half," someone will say. That's wonderful, but you don't want to be with half a person, and another person won't want to be with half of you. Any relationship, whether it's a friendship or romantic partnership, shouldn't be one of codependency, where one person (or both people) needs the other to fill a void in his/her life. Instead, let's strive to complete ourselves.

In creating a joyful life by ourselves, we naturally magnetize ourselves to attract others who share similar values. This is what is meant by the saying *your vibe attracts your tribe*. Living an authentic life that creates true joy within you is the best (and fastest) way to meet others who align with your message and your values. Let them be part of your growth, and allow one another the gift of collaborative progression.

Time and priorities.

Next time you are tempted to say that you don't have enough time for something, replace the latter half of the statement with "because it's not a priority" and see how it feels. For example: "I don't go to the doctor because my health is not a priority." Or: "No, honey, I can't help you with rewriting your resume because your resume is not a priority." Of course you have enough time for anything you want to do—your life is just moment after moment, strung together with passing seconds.

This realization shouldn't make you feel bad. In fact, it should empower you, because it's related to the idea that we often feel like we have to explain ourselves for wanting or not wanting to do something. If all we have is an undefined amount of time here, why shouldn't we occupy it as we'd like? Notice opportunities to defend or explain yourself, and then choose not to. Instead, turn within and sense the texture of misunderstanding. Just be with what is, instead of opting to ease it by explaining or defending. Don't get caught up in being right or wrong—you know what is right or wrong for you. You can do as you wish without being focused on the outcome. All you have to do is *just be.*

Can you feel the light within you? Did certain parts of this article strike a chord inside you somewhere? That's because you already know these things as truth, so don't let those truths be smothered by fear of what is not.

You may have a long list of resolutions or goals that you believe will provide you with happiness or contentment when they're attained or achieved, but if you examine your state of happiness in this moment, you'll realize that the fulfillment of your previous ambitions didn't create an eternal sense of joy.

If you do nothing else this year, I hope you bring happiness to every encounter in your life, instead of expecting external events to produce it for you. By staying in harmony with the natural, positive flow of life, all the contentment you could ever dream of will begin to flow into your experiences. You will meet the right people, the financial means to get where you're headed, and all of the necessary factors will come together to fulfill your wildest dreams.

Relax. Stop pushing yourself, and feel awe for everything that already is. *Just be.*

8

This Year, I'm Giving Myself Another Chance

Dian Tinio

This year, I am forgiving myself. For all my shortcomings, for all my mistakes, for all the things I did and regret doing. I am forgiving myself for all the times I let my guard down and was hurt. I am forgiving myself for all the times I fell for all the wrong people, for all the times I let my pride be bigger than my relationships. I am forgiving myself for all the people and relationships I allow to slip away, for all the people I took for granted. I am forgiving myself for all the hearts I broke, for all the souls I left crying in the middle of the night. I am forgiving myself for all the times I dreamed and failed, the moments I strived and was not enough. I am forgiving myself for all the bad choices I've made, for my past, for the part of me that was ugly and horrible.

This year, I am trying again. Despite of all the times I have fallen short, I will rise. I will overcome. This coming year, I am dreaming again. I am setting goal again, for myself, for my future, for the people I love. I am conquering odds once more, I am setting sail into the unknown. I am going out there, not knowing the possible results, but will just try. This year, I am coloring my blueprints and doing the best that I can to make this life worth looking back at after, say five years.

This year, I am believing again. I am believing in myself, that there is beauty inside me, that I am my own sunshine, that I am a work of art. I am believing that I can do the things I've always wanted to do. I am believing that despite all my imperfections and frailties, I am able. This coming year, I am believing again in people, that there are people with good intentions, with kind hearts. That there are people who actually want to love me for all I am, flaws and dirt considered. I am believing that there are true people who will stay by my side amidst the storm, through the tough days and even the easy ones. I am believing that people can be authentic and gracious, just like how I believe that I can be as well. That altogether, we can make it easier to live this life.

This year, I am going to be honest with myself, with people. Enough with the disguises, facades and the lies, if I'm not okay, I'm going to say it. If I don't like something, I am going to be vocal about it. I am going to be honest with life, with what I want, with what I feel–who knows, maybe life will be amiable enough to actually give it to me. I am going to be brutally true, with the people I keep, with the people I love, with my actions and my thoughts.

This year, I am letting myself flourish and just be who I want

to be. Away from all my own expectations. I am letting myself fly without controlling who I should be or who I should love. I am allowing myself the time and space I need in order to become. I am letting myself go. I am letting it take risks, climb mountains, jump leaps, overcome waves.

This year, I am recognizing myself and bringing credits to where credit is due. Because for what it's worth, after everything that happened last year, I deserve an applause. Not because I was amazing or great, but simply because I was able to set foot into this new year. Simply because I didn't let the tide flow through and drown me. Simply because I didn't let the collision scatter me into a million tiny pieces. Simply because I was stronger than my struggles, I was bolder than my battles, I was fiercer than my faults.

As this year begins, I want to start anew. I want to redeem myself. I want to have life, once more.

And, this year, this year is my revival.

And I believe it's yours, too.

9

I Hope In The New Year You Say No To Douchebags

Lauren Jarvis-Gibson

I hope this year, you have the strength to say no to men who only want one thing.

I hope in this new year, you realize your self-worth. **And I hope you realize that you deserve SO much more than a shitty guy who only sees you as a body part, and not as a human being.**

I hope in this new year, you come to the realization that you have been fucked over one too many times. And I hope you realize that at this point in your life, the sex isn't worth it. The empty hand holding isn't worth it. The sinister kisses aren't worth it and the diluted 'I love yous' honestly don't mean a thing.

And I hope you come to the realization that you deserve real love. Not the kind that is fleeting. Not the kind of love that leaves. Not the kind of love that is half-hearted.

I hope you know that you deserve a love that is 100%.

This new year, you deserve something that is bigger than yourself. You deserve the kind of love that lifts you up. The kind of love that is loving to all your flaws and all of your imperfections. The kind of love that is adoring and authentic in every way.

I hope you find the courage to wave goodbye to your past. I hope you find the courage inside of your heart to give yourself something that is beautiful, instead of something that will be gone tomorrow morning.

I hope you can hold onto hope, that one day you will get that great, big love that you have been praying for. And I hope you can do away with those men who whisper sweet nothings into your ear only to get into your pants. I hope you can do away with those men who only smile at you in order to get a kiss from you. I hope you can do away with those men who only compliment you when they are lonely, and those men who only text you at 2 am after a drunken night out.

You are not a piece of meat. You are not a single body part. You are not just a pair of breasts or a pair of shiny legs. You are not an object, and you don't deserve to be objectified.

You are a human being. You have a beating heart that has been through hell. You have a pair of lungs that have been through the ringer and have almost collapsed with your countless amount of heartbreaks. You have a soul. A soul that deserves nourishment and encouragement. Not broken promises and false hope.

I hope you know that you deserve more than you think you do. And you don't need those men in your life, those men who only look at your body instead of in your eyes or those men who only look forward to a night with you, instead of a morning loving you.

In this new year, please, say goodbye to douchebags, to fuck boys, and to people who have let you down in the past. And say hello to true love. **And know that no matter how long it takes, it is worth waiting for. I promise. You will find him one day. Don't stop hoping. Don't stop believing.**

10

25 Personal Milestones To Celebrate From This Year That Have Nothing To Do With Getting Married

Kim Quindlen

1. Having a rough week at work or in your personal life and still getting out of bed anyway, because you have trained yourself to be the kind of person that shows up.

2. Asking for a raise at your job, if you felt that you had worked hard and truly deserved it.

3. Finally making up with a friend you haven't had a relationship with for a long time.

4. Figuring out how to ask for (and get) help if you struggled with anxiety, depression, or any other challenge to your mental health at some point this year.

5. Finally being the one to buy your parents dinner, instead of the other way around. Even if you still just barely paid your credit card bill that month.

6. Moving into an apartment completely on your own, with no roommates or significant others or parents. Your couch, your spoons, your bathroom cleaning products, your everything.

7. Paying attention to the world around you, and actually making an effort this year to keep up with current events, the election, international affairs, and the news in general.

8. Running a marathon.

9. Completing a DIY project that had been bookmarked on your laptop for five months.

10. Learning how to enjoy your own company, and understanding that spending a Friday night by yourself can actually be an incredible thing.

11. Training yourself to actually confront someone when they've done something to hurt you or upset you, instead of just being passive aggressive towards them and avoiding the conflict.

12. Never forgetting to send out thank you notes–for a gift, for dinner, or just for someone's time.

13. Eating less salt, or less sodium, or less sugar, or less of whatever has been making you not feel your best.

14. Discovering a cause that's truly important to you and beneficial to others, and giving to it in some way–through your money or your time or your voice.

15. Getting on a plane even if you were terrified out of your mind.

16. Getting back into, or just beginning, an exercise regimen after avoiding it for so long.

17. And actually sticking to it.

18. Ending a relationship in which you weren't being treated the way you deserved to be treated.

19. Doing something kind for someone else and never telling anyone about it.

20. Traveling somewhere by yourself.

21. Or just finally forcing yourself to go on that trip you've talked about going on for years.

22. Learning how to cook a meal for yourself that was outside of your typical range.

23. Taking a class just for the fun of it.

24. Putting your health before your job.

25. Learning how to be kind to yourself, and good to yourself–even if it's a constant work in progress.

11

13 Positive Things You Need To Be Reminded Of As You Head Into The New Year

Nataliia Totka

1. Don't force it. Any of it. Be it friendships, relationships, perfect ponytails, life, people to be in your life, to write you, to understand you, to respond with respect. If they don't want to do that in the first place, you will only hurt yourself by trying to make it work. It won't. And you are better off.

2. Run away if you want. It's ok. Really. It is a-OK. I've been running away since I can remember. It comes to a halt at some point. But if you want to run, run. Don't let anyone stop you. You'll find yourself somewhere on the road, like Kerouac. Or you won't. Nobody knows.

3. Don't chase people. If they want to stay in your life, they will. Don't beg them to stay. Wish them well and let go. Though sometimes you should fight for what you want, a lot of those times you better let go. They will come back if it's kismet.

4. Know that everything changes. No-brainer. Feelings change. People change. Your self-worth changes. Your points of view change as well. Give it time and see how it goes. You might change.

5. Know that there is a blessing in every failure. You just don't know it yet. Failure is always a stinking disguise for something more. Be it a lesson, a better opportunity, an obstacle to see how much you want it, a masochistic device to get you in the mood for more. Don't make it negative. No need to curse or imprecate your offender. Bear with it.

6. Celebrate the small things. Do something small today that will lead you to a better life tomorrow. Make breakfast in bed. Pick up the book your girlfriend wants so much. Take him by surprise. Leave a cute note on the fridge.

7. Trust your gut. Or don't. Depends on how dependable your gut is.

8. Say what you want. Don't ever start a sentence with "I don't want…" or "I hate when you…", "I'd rather you didn't…" The more you say that the more it'll stick with you. Express your needs. Not what you'd hate to have.

9. Find your true self. It might be on the other continent, it might be in the woods with no cell reception. It might be in marketing, researching, or being the hot-shot CEO of your own company. Go and find it.

10. Your journey is yours and yours only. Don't compare yourself to others. Compare yourself to yourself. How are you better today? What changed in the last year? Are you the person you want to be? Or have you been very naughty this year?

11. Let more good things into your life. Think good thoughts. Read good books, have a cup of coffee or tea and chat with your colleague. Love. Build strong and lasting friendships, be adamant, be better. Be yourself.

12. Learn. "Live and learn" as they say. You'll go through heartbreak, depression, low self-esteem, you'll loose people you love or lost already, you'll be in a rut so many times you'd think that's the place to be. But you'll get to the other side and enjoy the rays of sunshine, it will all pass and life will be bright and full of promise. Until the next thing happens. You have what it takes to resolve anything that falls on your lap.

13. Know that you will be fine. It is painful to live sometimes; life isn't worth getting out of the bed every so often. Once in a while life is shit. And once upon a time there was a fairy tale and they supposedly lived happily ever after, maybe you can as well? Maybe we all can. With occasional grinds.

12

15 Beautiful John Green Quotes And The New Year's Resolutions You Should Make From Them

Colleen George

1. "Maybe there's something you're afraid to say, or some-one you're afraid to love, or somewhere you're afraid to go. It's gonna hurt. It's gonna hurt because it matters."

In the coming year, say what you feel and do what you know you need to do, even if you are afraid, and even if you are scared of getting hurt. It matters.

2. "It's very sad to me that some people are so intent on leaving their mark on the world that they don't care if that mark is a scar."

Spread goodness and light, and leave people better than you found them this year. Make your mark a mark of elegance and grace, filled with compassion and love.

3. "We need never be hopeless because we can never be irreparably broken."

Promise to always, always, always keep faith this year, and know that things will get better.

4. "I don't know a perfect person. I only know flawed people who are still worth loving."

This year, try not to be so critical of the people you hold near to you. They are only human, and they are trying. Try your best to value their love above the mistakes they may make because if you do, you will learn how to love even more fully.

5. "The town was paper, but the memories were not."

Stay in the moment—when you are with your friends, be with your friends. The rest of the details will disappear in time, but the memories of the good times—these will be cherished forever.

6. *"It is so hard to leave—until you leave. And then it is the easiest goddamned thing in the world."*

Allow yourself to learn to say goodbye. Allow yourself to accept what is best left in the past, or what is no longer serving you.

7. *"So here's my advice: study broadly and without fear. Learn a language if you can, because that will make your life more interesting. Read a little bit every day. But more importantly, surround yourself with people who you like and make cool stuff with them. In the end, what you do isn't going to be nearly as interesting or important as who you do it with."*

This year, cherish your relationships. Love each other a little bit more. Spend meaningful time with wonderful friends. Who you are with is more important than what you do.

8. *"At some point, you just pull off the Band-Aid. And it hurts but then it's over and you're relieved."*

You can do it. Whatever it is that needs to be done, you can do it. Even though sometimes it hurts, you will grow. Don't ignore what needs to be done simply out of fear of being hurt. You are incredibly resilient. Be brave this year.

9. *"Maybe it won't work out. But maybe seeing if it does will be the best adventure ever."*

Be a little more fearless this year. Take risks for the fun of the risk. You have no idea how it's going to turn out, but at least part of it is going to be spectacular. So you might as well see what happens.

10. *"That's always seemed so ridiculous to me, that people want to be around someone because they're pretty. It's like picking your breakfast cereals based on color instead of taste."*

Don't allow yourself to be distracted by glamourous appearances—whether it is money, a person, a job, or a lifestyle. True beauty and true happiness are both internal. This year, let go of whatever you are holding onto externally in order to create a life that is beautiful on the inside.

11. *"The only way out of the labyrinth of suffering is to forgive."*

This year can be your year of forgiveness and compassion. Forgive others, and please—forgive yourself. Mistakes occur and they are only human. Suffering occurs, yet it is always temporary. Forgive yourself, love, and you will find a whole authentically beautiful world at your feet.

> 12. *"And when people try to minimize your pain, they are doing you a disservice. And when you try to minimize your own pain you're doing yourself a disservice. Don't do that. The truth is that it hurts because it's real. It hurts because it mattered. And that's an important thing to acknowledge to yourself. But that doesn't mean that it won't end, it won't get better. Because it will."*

When things are hard this year, don't push them away—don't shy away in fear. Your feelings are here for a reason. Allow yourself to feel them and listen to them while remembering that things always have a way of getting better. This year, hold on to the wisdom that even when times are rough, you have the courage and strength to continue moving forward.

> 13. *"When you acknowledge that there is nothing repulsive or unforgivable or shameful about yourself, it becomes easier to be that authentic person and feel like you're living a less performed life."*

Finally, learn to forgive yourself this year. Be gentler on yourself and realize that your value is inherent within you—you, as a marvelous human being, have nothing to be ashamed of. Each day is an opportunity to reinvent yourself. You have 365 fresh canvases waiting at your fingertips—don't hold onto past mistakes as they are no longer relevant.

14. *"You don't get to choose if you get hurt in this world...but you do have some say in who hurts you. I like my choices."*

If you find that you truly value and respect someone, go ahead and love that someone. It's worth the risk. It's worth the chance.

15. *"As long as we don't die, this is gonna be one hell of a story."*

Here comes the New Year: get out there and live it up.

13

The 10 New Year's Resolutions That Will Guarantee Your Best Year Yet

Erica Gordon

The best part about the New Year is that it's a clean slate. There's a sense of comfort in leaving the past behind, feeling encouraged to let bad habits end with last year, and becoming motivated to make positive changes in the New Year.

The reason why New Year's resolutions can actually work is because there's something about a fresh start that not only drives us to be better but *reminds* us that it's possible to wipe our slate clean and change our ways.

The mentality behind "a New Year equals a fresh start" is incredibly powerful and motivating. There's a reason why January is the busiest month of the year at your local gym. People are more likely to take action and put in the effort towards achieving their goals when something external has represented a new beginning.

The best thing you can do is make specific New Year's resolutions, rather than just make a mental note that you'd like to "exercise more often" or "spend more time with the family". Here are 10 New Year's Resolutions that will guarantee your best year yet in the New Year:

1. Put your phone down during life's important moments.

Millennials are missing out on what's all around them due to a decision to observe life through a small screen. How can you fully enjoy a special occasion if you're on your phone documenting it via Snapchat and Instagram the entire time? Justin Wells of Westwind Recovery points out that social media addiction is a serious problem:

> *"Rather than taking in a special moment, millennials feel compelled to continually document almost every aspect of their lives, which significantly minimizes the enjoyment of any particular momentous occasion."*

If you learn to put down the phone during memorable moments, you'll take in and enjoy what's happening so much more. When you're on vacation at a stunning mountain resort, take it all in and keep the phone in your hotel room for a few hours while you go out exploring with just your eyes. When you're out with friends, enjoy their company by putting the phone down. In general, your best year yet will be the New Year if you can break your addiction to your smartphone.

2. Pursue your passion.

One of the most important goals to have is to work towards a career that involves you using your gift and pursuing your passion. A great goal to have for the New Year that will help you work towards your dream job is to start a passion project. A passion project can help you stay focused on your passion, practice your skills and use your gift in order to keep you on track and to keep you motivated.

3. Get your finances in order.

Getting your money in order can lead to financial freedom, which is integral to a happy and healthy life. You must be specific with your financial goals, though. Rather than telling yourself you want to "save more money" in the New Year, you must instead lay out specific expensive habits that you want to cut down on and have a goal in mind as to how much of each paycheck you want to put into a savings account.

Getting your finances in order also means paying your bills on time, managing your credit card balances, and caring about your credit. In a recent Capital One credit confidence study, over 70 percent of the 2,300 respondents maintained a belief that having good credit is the gateway to the "American Dream."

If you want to improve your credit, and you're dedicated to this New Year's Resolution, then pay all of your bills on time. That means settling your phone bill, electricity, cable, car payments and other bills *before* their due date. Late payments could show up as negative activity on your credit profile, and too many delinquencies could significantly lower your credit score.

4. Find someone to be accountable to at the gym.

Every year, millions of people have "get fit" or "lose weight" at the top of their New Year's resolutions list. What you need in order to achieve this resolution, though, is a specific plan that will actually work. You need external accountability. You need someone to answer to, someone who keeps track of you and someone who motivates you.

A personal trainer, for example, is someone you will be accountable to. This is someone you won't cancel on. When I have a training session booked at Steve Nash, I know that it's not something I can duck out of it–even if I don't feel like going. I'm *accountable* to my trainer. Unlike a group fitness class, when you book a one-on-one session with your trainer, you can't exactly get away with pulling a no-show. If you have one specific weight loss resolution for the New Year, it should be to

5. Meal prep and watch your alcohol and drug intake.

If weight loss is one of your New Year's resolutions, exercise alone won't cut it, but don't start some silly diet in the New

Year. Instead, meal prep. It's the best way to ensure you won't eat crap. The reason we eat unhealthy fast food is because we suddenly realize we're starving and we have nothing prepared. Meal prep changes all that, and it's a great habit to get into come the New Year.

If you want to watch your weight, though, you'll have to watch your alcohol intake too. And monitoring your alcohol consumption is a great New Year's resolution in general–not just for the sake of saving calories. Just as smoking Marijuana has some health benefits, some might argue that a glass of red wine has health benefits also. Sure it does, but all in moderation. A glass of red wine every now and then won't hurt you, and neither will the odd joint. Binge drinking and all day stoner sessions, though, will. As long as you're mindful of what foods and substances you're putting into your body, you're on the right path.

6. Plan one solo trip each year.

Even if it's just a weekend away to a nearby ski lodge, solo trips are fundamental to personal growth. You need time away, by yourself, on your mountaintop to re-charge, get creative and get inspired. If you can, plan an extended trip somewhere by yourself in the New Year, and use that valuable time to focus on your wants and needs.

7. Get out of your comfort zone and take advantage of opportunities.

Be more social, learn new skills, attend meet-ups and stop hiding out at home. Many of us feel that we're safer when nobody can see us and that's why we stay in so much. However, getting out of the house (and therefore getting out of your comfort zone) more often will truly pay off. Opportunities can get you everywhere, but they won't fall into your lap. You'll have to get outside, meet new people and experience more of life in order to run into beneficial, life-altering opportunities.

8. Be less of a couch potato.

Prolonged sedentary periods are bad for your well-being and bad for your health. In the New Year, try to watch less TV and be more active instead. Instead of pressing that "continue watching" button on Netflix, go to the gym instead. Find excuses to be active whenever you can. If a friend invites you out for dinner to catch up, suggest going for a walk together and catching up that way instead. You'll feel better at the end of each and every day if you were active that day.

In fact, get off the couch and make a point of getting outside every evening–at least for half an hour. You should commit to spending time in nature every single day because studies have proven that spending time in nature is linked to happiness, higher self-esteem, and a reduction in depression and anxiety. It's important to spend time away from TV screens and laptop screens because too much screen-time is incredibly bad for your well-being.

9. Tidy up and revamp your home.

The New York Times Bestseller, *The Life-Changing Magic of Tidying Up: The Japanese Art of Decluttering and Organizing* is a brilliant book that explains why tidying up and redecorating inspires a healthier overall mindset. It can even cure anxiety problems and help us feel more relaxed, as though a weight has been lifted. If you take the time to read that book, tidy up your space, and get more organized, the positive effects of this won't go unnoticed.

10. Practice gratitude and positivity.

There's a famous quote by Maltbie D. Babcock that sums it up wonderfully: "Better to lose count while naming your blessings than lose your blessings counting your troubles." So instead of focusing on what you don't have, focus your energy on gratitude towards what you *do* have. You'll make yourself miserable comparing yourself to others or focusing on the negative all the time. Just as easy as it is for you to complain about what's going wrong, it's equally easy to celebrate what's going right. The choice is yours, and the positive mindset instead of the negative one will guarantee your best year ever. As soon as you learn how to be more grateful, your whole life could change–not just your year.

14

11 Ways To Be A Better Person This Coming Year

Ari Eastman

1. Forgive yourself for the mistakes you've made in the past.

Resentment, be it with others or the self, builds itself into a toxic monster. It can invade our thinking, how we interact with the world, and ultimately, can keep us from achieving true peace. We're always told to forgive other people when they hurt us—to practice being the bigger person. But this can also be applied to the self. Forgive yourself for things that you've done. Forgive yourself for screwing up.

2. Give as often as you receive.

I believe generosity is a learned skill. Some will be born more inclined to it, but there's a reason we teach kindergartners the importance in sharing. The more you practice it, the easier it will come.

3. Listen. Listen. Listen.

I struggle with talking over people. It's a terrible habit that I have to actively remind myself to fight against. But it's so important. We don't listen to each other nearly enough. Even if we're not the one talking, we get wrapped up in what we're thinking or going to say and end up not being as engaged as we should be. This year, try to truly listen. Maintain eye contact. Respond accordingly to what the other person said instead of rushing to say something about yourself or your life.

4. Move your body.

If you're physically able, try to move your body every single day. Exercise isn't just about losing weight or getting that bullshit ~*~beach body~*~, it's about health and overall wellness. Get those endorphins going on a regular basis and you're likely to be a happier, more satisfied person. After all, remember in *Legally Blonde* when Elle says, "Exercise gives you endorphins. Endorphins make you happy. Happy people just don't shoot their husbands."

5. Set aside specific hours to unplug.

I love social media. I love the internet. So many amazing, bizarre opportunities have happened in my life because of it.

BUT, it can also drive. you. insane. Instead of refreshing your Twitter timeline incessantly, pick a few hours to do something that allows you to disconnect from online groupthink. Read a book. Go for a walk. Catch up with a friend. Journal. Whatever you enjoy!

6. Be accountable for your actions.

Going back to number 1, yes, I think it's good to forgive yourself for being imperfect. However, forgiveness doesn't cancel out accountability. There are consequences to what we do. Take ownership of what you do. It will not only make you a better person, it will also make you a more responsible member of society.

7. Embrace the weird parts of you.

We're actually all weirdos. We grow up thinking it's just us and we try to hide away anything that might make us *different*. But the thing is, EVERYONE has some quirk or bizarre aspect to their personality. I think that weirdness is what makes us interesting. So, don't shy away from what makes you stand out. Embrace it.

8. Try to learn a new perspective.

This does not mean abandoning what you believe in. This does not mean you have to listen to or validate someone who is demeaning you or your existence. But, there is value in trying to understand where another person is coming from.

9. Give back to your community.

Real talk: if every single person did something good, no matter how small, it would add up immensely. Find a cause you care about and research ways you can help. Maybe it's donating money, your time, or talents. Are you a social media guru? See if your favorite charity needs someone to help up their online presence. Are you a dope public speaker? Volunteer to emcee at an event. It's awesome to feel connected to something larger than just you.

10. Be honest in your romantic pursuits.

Are you just looking for casual sex? Boo, go get some. But, you know, be honest about it. Are you not interested in someone romantically? Gently let them down. Don't just disappear. You should always be honest about your intentions when another person becomes involved.

11. Love without holding back.

I get it. This is hard for a lot of us. It's natural to want to protect ourselves. We love people. They hurt us. We don't want that feeling again. So, we build walls. We push. We hide. In all honesty, I don't know how to fix it other than it's something you just have to start doing. Eventually it becomes, like anything else, a skill. Loving without reservations is one of the most thrilling things anyone can experience.

15

50 Important Questions To Ask Yourself As This Year Draws To A Close

Heidi Priebe

1. What made you feel the most alive this year?

2. How did you surprise yourself in this year?

3. What did you do this year that you regret?

4. What made you cry the hardest this year?

5. Which friends have been there for you the most in this year?

6. What are you most grateful for as this year draws to a close?

7. Compared to this time last year, are you happier or sadder?

8. What did you do to take care of yourself this year?

9. Where was the best place you traveled to this year?

10. What did you do for the first time in this year?

11. What did you do for the last time in this year?

12. Which days from this year will you never forget?

13. What did you accomplish this year that you're proud of?

14. Who did you need to forgive this year?

15. What were you most afraid of this year?

16. How did life surprise you this year?

17. How was this year better than last year?

18. How was this year worse than last year?

19. Who did you miss the most over the past year?

20. What was the most valuable thing you spent money on this year?

21. What did you waste too much money on this year?

22. How did you spend your birthday this year?

23. What was the best book you read in this year?

24. What do you wish you'd spent more time doing this year?

25. What do you wish you'd spent less time doing?

26. What made you the angriest in this year?

27. When did you feel the most at peace this year?

28. What is the biggest risk you took in this year?

29. What made you laugh the hardest this year?

30. What ended for you in this year?

31. What began for you in this year?

32. What song will always remind you of this year?

33. How did this year differ from the way you thought it would go?

34. How would you describe your personal style over the past year?

35. Who in your life did you look up to the most this year?

36. Which quote best sums up the past year for you?

37. Did you fall in love this year?

38. Did your heart break this year?

39. What was your favorite TV show in this year?

40. Which (if any) new years resolutions did you keep this year?

41. Which (if any) new years resolutions will you be making for next year?

42. What disappointed you the most in this year?

43. Who did you rely on the most in this year?

44. Who might you owe an apology to at the end of this year?

45. How did you grow as a person over the past year?

46. What made you feel the most stuck this year?

47. What made you feel the most inspired this year?

48. If you could go back and give yourself a single piece of advice on the first day of this year, what would it be?

49. What's the most important thing you learned this year?

50. What do you hope will be different for you by this time next year?

16

Here Is What I Hope For You In The New Year

Lacey Ramburger

I hope you take a look around at the people who have held you together for another year. Let's face it, even the most independent spirit needs a shoulder to lean on, and in the routine of day to day it's easy to forget that you've had people cheering you on and holding onto you on the days and nights where you couldn't even think of taking another step forward. Yet here you are, and so are they, and you are the luckiest person in the universe to be able to say that.

I hope you silently thank the people who walked out of your life this year. For one reason or another, not everyone stays—not just romantically, but in friendships too. Not every person you expect to stand by your side ends up coming through. Some people weren't intended to be in your story for the rest of your years, but temporary characters woven throughout your stories—to teach you lessons and make you a better person. And if they left your life, I hope you don't beat yourself up and carry it with you—but be grateful for the times you had together, and wish them well.

I hope you open your arms to new people. That you don't only decide that the faces you've come to know and the voices you're so used to hearing are the only ones that will ever matter. That you don't pass up the chance to say hi to that stranger who's reading the book you love, or to that person who you suspect you would get along with, but you're too afraid to make the first move. Make moves. Close the gaps between you and the people in this world. Remember that for every person in your life that you love so dearly, they were once a stranger too, and now you can't imagine life without them—so why not give others that chance too?

I hope you open your heart, too. Maybe you have someone who will be kissing you at midnight and holding your hand into this new year, and for that, be grateful. Yet over time we tend to stop exploring and believing there is anything left to discover in a person—we stop caring as much because we think we know everything. Take a look at this person, and look at their face—are they the same person you knew at the beginning? Discover them again, and again, and again. If you don't have your forever person, or any person at all, then I hope you open your heart as wide as you know how. That you don't allow past hurts and loves gone wrong to cause you to never try again. I hope you do the opposite—I hope you love without hesitation, without worrying they will break your heart—because let me tell you, everyone's going to break your heart a little. If you never open your heart, you will never find the love you deserve—so do it.

I hope you take chances—little ones, big ones, everything in between. Whether it's a simple change from your usual style that you've been too nervous to try, or it's an opportunity that changes your entire life—I hope you take it. I hope you don't allow past voices and the self-deprecating words in your head tell you that you're not worth it; that you don't let them keep you from going for dreams and chances you never thought possible. That you don't stay within the confines of comfort that you've used as an excuse to play it safe. That you see more than that in yourself, and that you do something about it.

I hope in the New Year, you surprise yourself with just how incredible you are.

17

I Hope You Live A Little Louder In This New Year

Marisa Donnelly

In this new year, I hope you do things that challenge you.

That trip to India that you have been dying to take, that side job you know will push your limits, or that coffee date with a loved one you haven't seen in years. I hope you do things that frighten you, like kiss the person who makes your heart flutter, or send that risky text, or reach out to an old friend and repair a broken relationship. It is in these hard moments that you grow the most, that you strengthen your heart, that you learn who you are and who you wish to become. So I hope you decide to challenge yourself in this new year. Your mind and your body are more powerful than you think.

In this new year, I hope you say yes.

Say yes to that date, say yes to that slice of chocolate cheesecake, say yes to that girls' weekend in Las Vegas or the boys' softball tournament in the city. Say yes to that new project at work. Say yes to something you never thought you would. Say yes to something that's probably going to end up terribly, but is still worth it for the experience and the lessons. Say yes because yes gives you opportunities. Say yes because saying yes is infinitely better than wondering what could have happened.

In this new year, I hope you let go.

I hope you stop holding onto people that have hurt you, or negative memories. I hope you learn to forgive those who have wronged you and try to see the good side in every situation, even if it looks like there isn't one. I hope you take a deep breath, then exhale all that isn't building you, strengthening you, or helping you become something better. In this new year, I hope you learn to heal. Because you deserve that.

In this new year, I hope you go after what you want.

Life is too short to wonder what could have been or to waste time chasing the wrong things. If it's a job you want or a person you love, if it's a future you've believed in or a dream you've been craving, *go after it*, fully and completely. I hope this year is one for selfish pursuits and confidence. I hope that all that you take steps forward where you were hesitant. I hope you stop holding back.

In this new year, I hope you are fearless.

I hope you stop second-guessing and questioning your decisions. I hope you stop wondering 'what if' and playing it safe. I hope you always use your head, but I hope you follow your heart, too. I hope you stop overthinking and analyzing all the results and instead just go forward. I hope you learn that fear is holding you back from who you could be, and you don't allow it to anymore.

In this new year, I hope you smile.

I hope you stop hanging onto negativity or letting darkness cloud your skies. I hope you find reasons to be happy, big or small, and carry those with you wherever you go. I hope you stop worrying about things you can't control or people you can't change. I hope you speak words of kindness to yourself and to others. In this new year, I hope you're happier.

In this new year, I hope you live louder.

I hope you laugh more. I hope you sing at the top of your lungs. I hope you drive with the windows down and let the wind rustle through your hair. I hope you hug. I hope you kiss. I hope you surround yourself with people who make you feel alive. I hope you become the type of person that brings good energy wherever you go, and the type of person people want to be around. I hope you speak what's on your mind, that you raise your voice for injustice, that you tell others that you love them, instead of waiting until it's too late. I hope you live louder, shine brighter. This is your year.

18

Do Yourself A Life-Changing Favor: Forget Your Past And Move On With Your Life

Mary McMahon

Wake up, it's a new year. You have this moment to brush off the last year of memories and start new. Sure, you could do this at any time of the year, but for me, there is nothing more refreshing that a global restart button to forget whatever the hell happened in the last 365 days. I'm sure, like most of the general population, you had a year with good and bad things that happened to you. Regardless, I'm sure a lot of things stuck with you through the years that you wish you could just forget. Well friend, I am here to tell you to reflect, take a deep breath, and let these things go before they overcome you.

Now, that's easier said than done, right? It's easier to *say* that you need to forget about every little thing that happened to you that caused you heartbreak, loss, or just general garbage feelings than it is to just *do* it. Because memories never forget. Memories make up who you are. But you can't let your past seep into your future and ruin any prospect of happiness that you have. You have to refuse to let this happen because your past is the only measure of time that can affect you fully.

And that is the worst part about the past.

It is the only thing that has an effect on both your present and future life. It is the only thing that follows you through every moment of your life. It's a little shadow that follows behind you, creeping up on you when you least expect it, to remind you that you are who you are because of it.

And sure, you can let it define your life. You can let it take over every single part of your soul. You can let it take hold of you. You can let it take away your individuality so that people only recognize you as "that person with that thing that had happened to them."

But do yourself a favor, and don't. Don't let yourself be that person who keeps their head in the mud. Don't drag the dead weight around everywhere you go through every experience because you can't possibly grow when you're stuck carrying around all that extra baggage. Pull an Elsa and let it go already.

Memories like falling in love, falling apart, and heartbreak can be the worst to shake. With love, it's an everlasting memory ingrained in your heart, in your mind, and in your soul. When you love someone, you can move on and even though the memory of that person's light and love will always stick with you, you can't let it define what your present state is. They will always be that memory of an unrequited, romanticized hologram of your past. But you can't let it bother you anymore. You can't let every moment with someone new be dictated by what happened in your past. You can't expect that the way someone has treated you in the past is the way that all people will treat you in the future.

Gain wisdom from that, not skepticism.

But I get it. Sometimes certain memories are harder to *just get over*. From what I find, the memories that have a deeper connection to your soul are the hardest to move past. Some memories are horrible. Some memories are so bad that you can't forget them. But I just ask that you don't let them define who you are. I ask you to be thankful for those moments because you are so much more than what they could define you as. You are so much more than an unfortunate memory. You are so much more than those few moments that forever changed your life.

And I guess that is the beautiful thing about the past. No matter how good or bad it is, it's shaped you to be the person you are today. You wouldn't be that person if you didn't have a series of events following your every footstep into the future.

Memories don't forget. Memories certainly won't forget you. But you can try to. You can try to use those memories not as a fault for caution, but as a tool to grow. Give yourself that gift this year.

19

I Hope In The New Year You Quit

Kirsten Corley

I hope in the New Year, you quit being afraid and finally go after that thing that scares you.

I hope you quit hanging on to the past and letting it interfere with the present.

I hope in the New Year, you quit settling and wait for what you deserve, even if that means waiting a long time.

I hope you quit hating yourself and fixating upon flaws you can't change. I hope you look at your reflection with the admiration it deserves.

I hope in the New Year, you quit doing something that doesn't make you happy even if you don't know what does yet.

I hope you quit a job you hate even if that means you'll be broke for a little while.

I hope in The New Year, you quit bad company and begin to surround yourself with people who enhance your life and make it better.

I hope you quit that relationship that isn't going anywhere.

I hope in The New Year, you quit living up to other people's expectations of how you're supposed to live your life.

I hope you quit killing yourself to makes others happy and start trying to make yourself happy.

I hope in the New Year, you quit lying to yourself about what you really want and find the courage to go after it.

I hope you quit comparing yourself to others and start by comparing yourself to the person you were yesterday.

I hope in The New Year, you quit running from love and let it find you.

I hope you quit thinking you're in a rush to get somewhere and learn to appreciate the moment.

I hope in The New Year, you quit walking down the path of someone else's choosing and go after your dreams, no matter how crazy they might be.

I hope you quit being stressed. You quit feeling pressure. I hope you find the core to what is causing these feelings and simply quit.

I hope in The New Year, you quit holding onto your ex because it's over and you need to quit thinking he'll come back.

I hope you quit needing people and learn to love yourself and your company.

I hope in The New Year, you quit going out when you'd rather stay in and not feel bad about it.

I hope you quit looking back and dwelling over where you were and start focusing on where you are going.

I hope in The New Year, you quit waking up unhappy and find what it is that will make you want to get out of bed in the morning.

But most of all I hope you quit holding yourself back.

Quit tolerating less than you deserve. Quit settling. Quit living someone else's life. Simply quit.

Quit until you're leading a life that fills you with such joy and happiness you wish you found the courage to quit sooner.

20

101 Life Lessons I'm Taking With Me Into The New Year

Priscilla Anais Vazquez

1. Nightmares can come true just as much as dreams do if you let your fears guide you internally.

2. When you are busy, your heart will shout things to you and you may ignore these cries for help. These screams will be likely to show up in your more subconscious dreams as skits.

3. Mistakes are a blessing because they help you grow.

4. Any mentor in your life who aggravates you may be an angel sent to you in disguise.

5. Everything happens FOR you, not to you.

6. When you ignore your gut instinct, the same burning truth gets exposed to you a second time.

7. There will always be someone to disagree with you, especially if your idea is bigger than their typical thought process.

8. We are all searching for things we already have.

9. You get what you generally give.

10. Reflect after reacting.

11. Don't ever beg for someone to want you the way that you want them.

12. Continue growing or people will grow out of you.

13. What you see with your eyes does not tell every detail of every story.

14. Being impulsive is a choice to fulfill your own urge of release without considering other people's feelings.

15. People can care about you to an extent and will give you advice on survival but only you can give yourself the things that your heart harasses you about throughout your day(s).

16. Most of the time people do mean what they say but feelings change.

17. Space is necessary and should be embraced.

18. Time and space can will give you the answers you've been looking for.

19. Holding on can be more painful than letting go.

20. Everything and everyone contributes to our roads of self-discovery.

21. Self-discovery is offered to us in many different situations or conversations.

22. Certain people trigger certain traits of yourself.

23. There is a little bit of you in everyone. Everyone has a little bit of you.

24. A lot of things wouldn't bother you if you didn't focus on how someone else might feel. (Guilt)

25. Some people just stop talking to you because you remind them of someone they are trying to forget. You can't control that.

26. Some people use you for comfort then secretly disappear and that doesn't make them the Satanic. You helped them grow or realize something.

27. Some people want to be used for their comfort to feel more like a value of importance or a part of something big. It's like being a hero.

28. Healthy relationships help motivate structure. (This can be a romantic relationship but most importantly, the relationship you have and maintain with yourself.)

29. Abusive relationships show you the things about yourself that you need to work on.

30. Abusive relationships also test your will power and resilience.

31. Everything is perception.

32. Everything you say or declare which is right, is indeed correct.

33. Be careful with what you solidify.

34. People generally want something to complain about.

35. People want to hear you complain because "misery loves company."

36. The people that only come alive when you talk negatively are toxic people. (Hypothetically they may or may not see themselves as a hero to save you and that can be linked to having low self-esteem.)

37. People with low self-esteem feel useful when they are the one(s) that are there for you when no-one else is.

38. A person who will bring up how they were there for you when nobody else was to win an argument or feel superior (just because they are not quickly receiving what they want from you) is typically committing abusive behavior.

39. You can disrespect someone or degrade someone without using actual curse words.

40. You can be superior in your life without insulting others.

41. Most work industries promote the opposite of what they truly are about daily.

42. Some people end up being what you made them out to be.

43. We all need an outlet.

44. Art is everywhere, as well as inspiration.

45. The world is not black and white. It's multi-colored and has colors you don't even know the names of.

46. It is not just the message you are delivering, it's the way you deliver the message because your tone matters.

47. One sentence can ruin or taint a bond permanently.

48. An alcohol or drug addiction can be at a mild level or an extreme level. (You might not need a shot of tequila in the morning but you might think you need 4-6 glasses of wine every night.)

49. We can reward ourselves in creative and sober ways.

50. I cannot speak for everyone and list every reason but sometimes we become addicted to substances because we feel like we have nobody open-minded enough to talk to.

51. Drugs can help us take a short-cut into our subconscious.

52. What you don't want to hear is what you may need to hear.

53. We don't realize how much our words and actions can affect others.

54. With some people, the less you are around them, the better.

55. People warn you about other people but in the end, we are all people.

56. Assumptions are a short cut instead of directly asking.

57. You become what you obsess over.

58. You become who you hate.

59. You become your thoughts.

60. You can make yourself sick.

61. Sometimes when you see someone directly go into another relationship after leaving their last relationship, you may view it as fast or "jumping" but don't forget that people stay in relationships after they don't want to anymore. The process of getting over someone was probably already happening during the relationship.

62. We are given the opportunity every second to create ourselves into a whole new person.

63. Some of us are addicted to drama at a certain level and don't fully realize it.

64. Sometimes you don't need to think a long time to decide because your heart and/or gut already knew the answers.

65. I consider "friends" a distraction if our goals are not similar or if they do not stimulate my growth.

66. Learning is an unlimited process.

67. You can be 42 and learn something new from a 7-year-old. You just need to be humble enough to listen.

68. If you are not humble enough then situations will occur in your life to bring you back down to earth and that is why I said up above that "Everything happens for you, not to you."

69. Gods are always trying to send you messages.

70. Sometimes it's easier to tell a stranger your biggest secrets.

71. Someone you've only known for three days can break your heart.

72. Someone you just met can do more for you than someone you've known your whole life.

73. The universe thrives off energy so drink coffee and get shit done.

74. When alcohol or weed is in your system, it gives you vague or false perceptions of a bond with someone that FEELS real.

75. If you don't take responsibility for your actions and play victim, then you will stay a victim of your life. You will stay the passenger seat of you're the vehicle you finance.

76. Blaming others for your life's circumstances is the easy way out.

77. Being drunk once felt fun because it helped me procrastinate.

78. Alcohol helped me accept the things I haven't accomplished yet and made me okay with it.

79. Try not to make any important decisions under the influence of any external substance.

80. Everything connects and everything matters.

81. We either have multiple soul mates depending on who we're becoming or what's convenient for our life at the time or "Soul Mate" is merely a perception or fantasy and merely does not exist.

82. Eating clean helps me listen to my body and my mind more. (This is more of a realization.)

83. The person who tries to make the "bad guy" look like the "bad guy" most likely the bad guy.

84. Typically, females should take precautions because they are often victimized into situations where a male is in love with the idea of the female rather than her imperfections, growth, emotions and time.

85. Be in a relationship with someone who can admit when they're wrong, to make your life easier. If otherwise, prepare yourself for Emotional Hell and earlier gray hairs.

86. People will look for excuses to not be in a relationship if they truly do not want to be in one.

87. There are situations out there bigger than your feelings.

88. If you don't make your dreams come true, then you are more likely to resent your children or your spouse for your lack of action. (I am not saying this is right, I am just simply stating that I've seen it happen multiple times) For example, Mother says: "If I never had kids, I could have been a flight attendant."

89. Don't give a boy or a man your all, all at once. (A guy himself gave me this advice.)

90. Silence beats ignorance.

91. Too much silence creates assumptions, which creates tension and misunderstandings.

92. People tend to over rate themselves.

93. People respond better to love.

94. A high level of professionalism will attract business opportunities to you quickly.

95. Good memory is an advantage in the business world.

96. Writing things down improves memory.

97. If you don't start planning or decorating your life, then someone else will do it for you.

98. Whatever brings you happiness may not be the same recipe or formula for another person's joy.

99. We all have different callings.

100. We all typically categorize people by their words, tones and appearance because it seems easier than getting to know them within time.

101. We are given the opportunity every second to create ourselves into a whole new person.

21

For Anyone Who Already Feels Paralyzed In The New Year

Kim Quindlen

I have a love/hate relationship with the beginning of each new year.

I love the feeling of having a fresh start, a rebirth, a clean slate. Each time December draws to a close, the excitement in the air is tangible. People are ready to start over, to do things differently, to wake up feeling like they are full of potential and free of burden.

I love reflecting back on the twelve months I just lived—patting myself on the back for the things I achieved, and reminding myself that tomorrow is a new day when I think about all of the ways that I failed. The new year is a reassurance that the world is always turning, that you are free to keep trying and keep chasing after what you want. As endless and overdone as they are, I love the abundance of articles on how to live your best life this year. I love hearing about people's New Year's Resolutions. I love the endless TV programs and listicles and videos reflecting back on the year and looking towards what's to come. I love the hope, the uncertainty, the excitement, the promise that hangs in the air.

But every time a new year begins, I'm also paralyzed.

I think of all the things I didn't do last year. I add them to the list of all of the things I want to do this year. I do the math in my head. I think about all the things I'm likely to fail at—some of them, for a second or third time. I think about my resolutions, my hopes for the future, and I wonder how they match up to everyone else's. Are mine stupid? Self-involved? Foolish? Worthy? Pointless? Impractical? Impossible? I'm suddenly overwhelmed with what I want to do, and how I could ever possibly get there. I stop thinking about the things I want to accomplish over the next few months and instead fall into a black hole of worry about where my life is going to go in the next ten years and how far behind I probably am in comparison to everyone else.

And then the new year, which is supposed to be so cleansing, refreshing, and rejuvenating, becomes a brick wall that falls on my chest and prevents me from moving in any direction—even just that of side-to-side. I can't move, because even just a small step becomes a possibility to fail, a possibility for my dreams to be crushed, a possibility of me looking foolish. Opportunity becomes terrifying instead of exciting. A clean slate becomes an alarming pit of emptiness reflecting back at me. A new year full of potential just becomes another place for my brain to set up camp and think of all the ways I can screw it up.

I add salt to the wound by thinking about all the things that my friends and family members did this year, all of their accomplishments, all the ways I am unworthy of the crowd I surround myself with. I long to go back to those joyful few days before the holidays, when I was wrapping presents, tying up loose ends before I took off work for a few days, and preparing to head home—too busy to think about the looming fresh start, the clean slate, the open abyss of opportunities that could either lead to success or failure.

But the holidays always fly by, and then January sits down heavily, staring into my face and daring me to make a move. The initial excitement and hope fizzles out, and I am left with the crushing pressure of my own expectations and self-reflections. But then, I remember that I was in this exact same spot last year. I felt the pressure, the strain, the crushing feelings of inadequacy. I thought about all the ways that I sucked, all the reasons that I should strive to just *get by* instead of coming up with goals and things that I wanted to accomplish. And then, day by day, I got over it, because I started thinking of the new year in exactly those terms—day by day. I stopped thinking about where I would be in April and September and December and started thinking about what I wanted to happen today, this week, this month.

I stopped listening to everybody else's goals for the new year, everybody else's accomplishments from the previous year. Their stories and their journeys and their opinions faded into the background. And I was just able to focus on me, and my little piece of notebook paper with the goals I had for the year. And how I could start working on those goals today, tomorrow, and next Tuesday, instead of worrying about exactly where I should be in eight months and three weeks from now.

It's normal to feel paralyzed with the start of a new year. It's normal to feel inadequate and stuck and lost. In reality, those feelings never fully go away. And the fear never fully goes away, either—you just learn how to chip away at it, one piece at a time. The people who are always the most successful are not the ones who entered each new year with clear eyes and a rock-solid amount of self-esteem and an iron-clad grip on their life plan. On the contrary, the most successful people in the world dealt with constant failure, rejection, and disappointment. But they learned how to rebound in spite of it, and to let that failure become a part of them in a good way, in a way that provided them with more wisdom and life lessons and the knowledge that failure will not kill you.

So if you're feeling paralyzed by the new year, stop thinking about the new year. Just think about today, and tomorrow, and the next day. Failure is inevitable, disappointment is inevitable. But the more you chip away at the stone of fear that lives in your stomach, the more you'll understand that its power is not as strong as yours.

YOU MIGHT ALSO LIKE:

All The Reminders You Need To Get Through Anything In Life
by Thought Catalog

Seeds Planted in Concrete by Bianca Sparacino

Being Whole by Lacey Ramburger

**THOUGHT
CATALOG
Books**

THOUGHT CATALOG

IT'S A WEBSITE.

www.thoughtcatalog.com

SOCIAL

facebook.com/thoughtcatalog
twitter.com/thoughtcatalog
tumblr.com/thoughtcatalog
instagram.com/thoughtcatalog

CORPORATE

www.thought.is

Printed in Great Britain
by Amazon

86492977R00066